PAYING THROUGH THE NOSE
AND OTHER ENGLISH EXPRESSIONS

by Andrew Niccol *pictures by* Stephen Woodman

SPHERE
SPHERE BOOKS LIMITED
30-32 Gray's Inn Road, London WC1X 8JL

First published in Great Britain by
Sphere Books Ltd 1983
Copyright © 1983 by Andrew Niccol
Cartoons copyright © 1983 by Stephen Woodman

TRADE
MARK

Reproduced, printed and bound in Great Britain by
Hazell Watson & Viney Ltd, Aylesbury, Bucks.

Making friends.

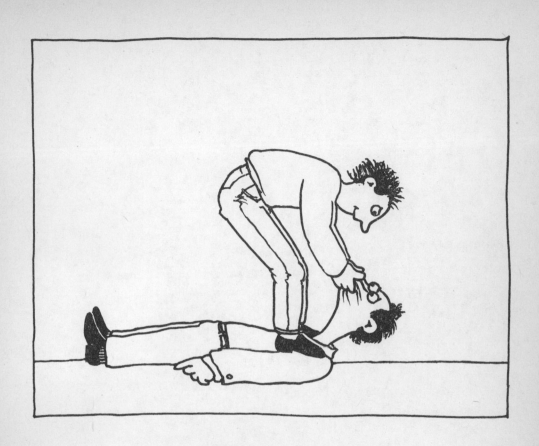

Pulling a face.

Catching a bus.

A fan club.

A face-lift.

Bringing up children.

Getting the sack.

A royal flush.

A half-brother.

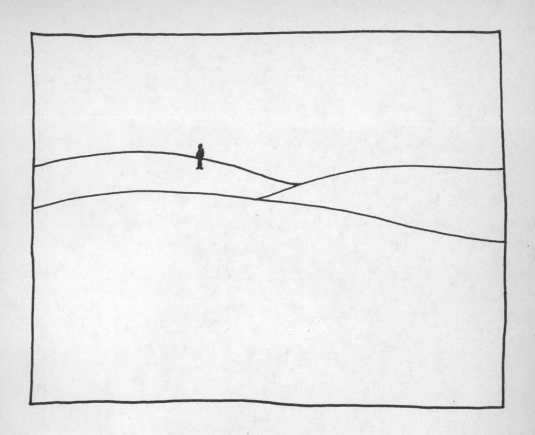

A distant cousin.

Taking a bath.

Putting a deposit on a house.

Toasting the bride.

Picking your nose.

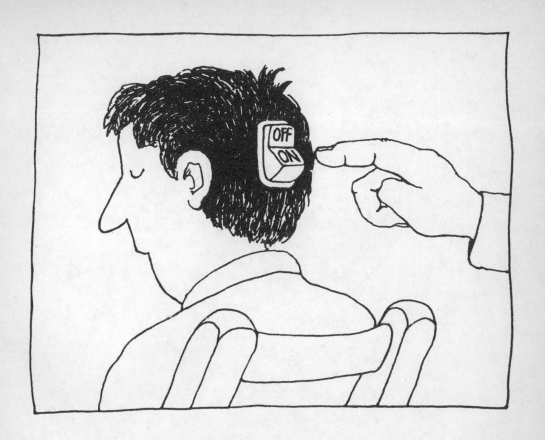

Turning someone on.

Weight watching.

Pinching someone's bottom.

Being on the pill.

A stag party.

A flash in the pan.

Walking the plank.

Making a pig of yourself.

Calling a spade a spade.

Passing the buck.

Baby-sitting.

A junk shop.

Shooting your mouth off.

Serving dinner.

Making mincemeat out of someone.

Crop-dusting.

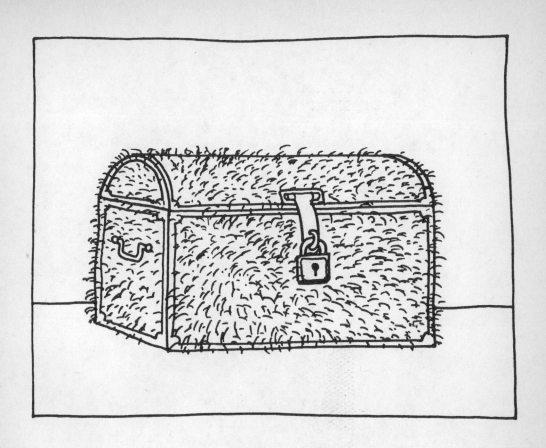

A hairy chest.

An armpit.

Paying through the nose.

Licking someone into shape.

Putting words in someone's mouth.

Breast feeding.

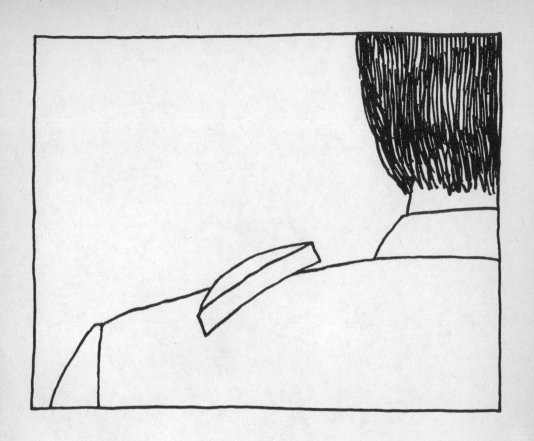

Having a chip on your shoulder.

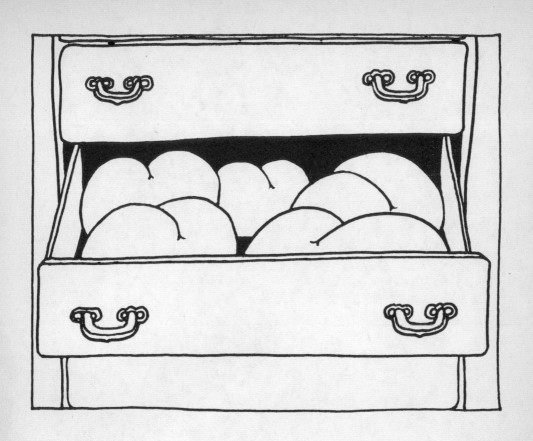

A bottom drawer.

A concentration camp.

Lying in bed.

Panel-beating.

Spring cleaning.

Brainwashing.

A beachcomber.

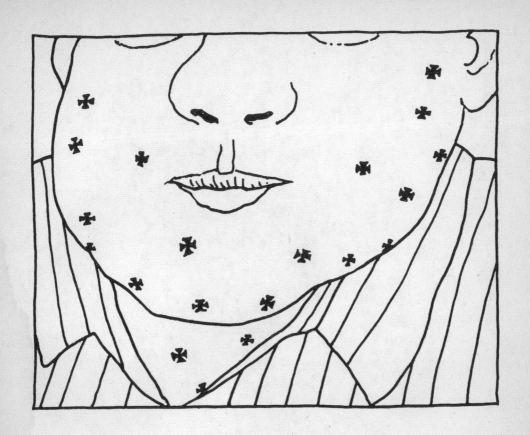

German measles.

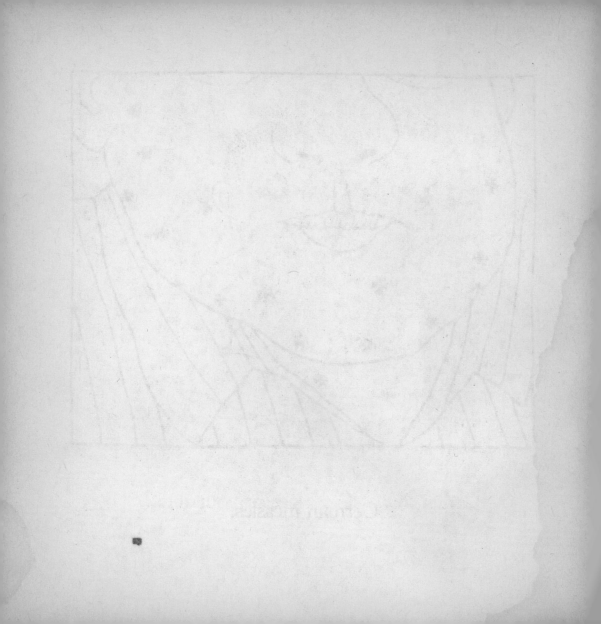

Giving someone a piece of your mind.